Other titles in the series:
The Victim's Guide to Air Travel
The Victim's Guide to The Baby
The Victim's Guide to Christmas
The Victim's Guide to The Dentist
The Victim's Guide to The Doctor
The Victim's Guide to Middle Age

Published simultaneously in 1995 by Exley Publications in
Great Britain and Exley Giftbooks in the USA.

12 11 10 9 8 7 6 5 4 3 2 1

Copyright © Roland Fiddy, 1995

ISBN 1-85015-626-3

A copy of the CIP data is available from the
British Library on request.

Printed in Spain by Grafo, S.A. – Bilbao.

Exley Publications Ltd, 16 Chalk Hill, Watford, Herts WD1 4BN,
United Kingdom.
Exley Giftbooks, 232 Madison Avenue, Suite 1206,
NY 10016, USA.

EXLEY
NEW YORK · WATFORD, UK

Do not be afraid of the boss ....

① ②

How to overcome your fear....

MANAGER

③

Underneath that stern exterior there
could be a vulnerable human being ....

Bosses like their staff to be considerate ....

... and committed ...

1.

2.

...but there is no need to be a creep!

It is important to establish who **IS** the boss....

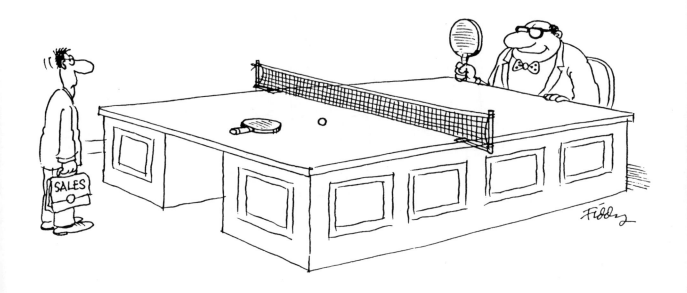

1

2

⑤

⑥

⑦

⑧

①

②

Points of View.

①

②

Remember — your boss did not reach his present position by worrying about his shortcomings......

... But he will be sure to notice YOURS!

①   ②   →

1. The Secret Life of a Business Tycoon.

2.

3.

4.

5.

➡

6.

7.

Books in the "Victim's Guide" series
($4.99   £2.99 paperback)

Award-winning cartoonist Roland Fiddy sees the funny side of life's phobias, nightmares and catastrophes.

The Victim's Guide to Air Travel
The Victim's Guide to The Baby
The Victim's Guide to The Boss
The Victim's Guide to Christmas
The Victim's Guide to The Dentist
The Victim's Guide to The Doctor
The Victim's Guide to Middle Age

Books in the "World's Greatest" series
($4.99   £2.99 hardback)

The World's Greatest Business Cartoons
The World's Greatest Cat Cartoons
The World's Greatest Dad Cartoons
The World's Greatest Do-It-Yourself Cartoons
The World's Greatest Golf Cartoons
The World's Greatest Keep-Fit Cartoons
The World's Greatest Marriage Cartoons
The World's Greatest Sex Cartoons

Books in the "Fanatics" series
($4.99   £2.99 paperback)

The **Fanatic's Guides** are perfect presents for everyone with a hobby that has got out of hand. Eighty pages of hilarious black and white cartoons by Roland Fiddy.

The Fanatic's Guide to the Bed
The Fanatic's Guide to Cats
The Fanatic's Guide to Computers
The Fanatic's Guide to Dads

The Fanatic's Guide to Diets
The Fanatic's Guide to Dogs
The Fanatic's Guide to Golf
The Fanatic's Guide to Husbands
The Fanatic's Guide to Money
The Fanatic's Guide to Sex
The Fanatic's Guide to Skiing
The Fanatic's Guide to Sports

Books in the "Crazy World" series
($4.99   £2.99 paperback)

The Crazy World of Aerobics (Bill Stott)
The Crazy World of Cats (Bill Stott)
The Crazy World of Cricket (Bill Stott)
The Crazy World of Gardening (Bill Stott)
The Crazy World of Golf (Mike Scott)
The Crazy World of The Handyman (Bill Stott)
The Crazy World of Hospitals (Bill Stott)
The Crazy World of Housework (Bill Stott)
The Crazy World of Learning to Drive (Bill Stott)
The Crazy World of Love (Roland Fiddy)
The Crazy World of Marriage (Bill Stott)
The Crazy World of The Office (Bill Stott)
The Crazy World of Photography (Bill Stott)
The Crazy World of Rugby (Bill Stott)
The Crazy World of Sailing (Peter Rigby)
The Crazy World of School (Bill Stott)
The Crazy World of Sex (David Pye)
The Crazy World of Soccer (Bill Stott)

Great Britain: Order these super books from your local bookseller or From Exley Publications Ltd, 16 Chalk Hill, Watford, Herts WDl 4BN. Please send £1.30 to cover post and packaging on 1 book, £2.60 on 2 or more books.)